GOD'S OFFICIAL

GOD'S OFFICIAL

A fantasy football fable

by Robert Farquhar

JOSEF WEINBERGER PLAYS

LONDON

God's Official
First published in 2002
by Josef Weinberger Ltd
12-14 Mortimer Street, London, W1T 3JJ

ISBN 0 85676 265 2

For Sue, Mary and George

GOD'S OFFICIAL was first performed at the Unity Theatre, Liverpool on January 18th 2000 by Peccadillo Theatre Company, with the following cast:

DEGSY   Eddie Chinn

CLIFF   Warren Donnelly

GREAVES   Gary Bowman

Directed by Robert Farquhar
Lighting by Tim Brown

GOD'S OFFICIAL was presented at the Pleasance Theatre, Edinburgh as part of the 2000 Edinburgh Festival Fringe on August 2nd 2000 and subsequently transferred to the Warehouse Theatre, Croydon from October 8th 2000 before an extensive UK tour. The play was produced by Sally Vaughan and Richard Jordan Ltd in association with Peccadillo Theatre Company, with the following cast:

DEGSY   Eddie Chinn

CLIFF   Warren Donnelly

GREAVES   Martyn Avery-Williams

Directed by Robert Farquhar
Lighting by Tim Brown

In November 2002 Richard Jordan Productions Ltd presented a new production of the play for a UK tour which included seasons at the West Yorkshire Playhouse and Stephen Joseph Theatre, Scarborough.

AUTHOR'S NOTE

In writing GOD'S OFFICIAL my intention is that there is no
indication who the actual relegated football team is. Obviously
the accents of the characters will give a huge clue as to who it
might be, and when we first performed the play it was with
Liverpool accents as that's where we're from. I would hope
that the play would work perfectly well played in any major
regional accent, eg Mancunian, Glaswegian, Geordie, etc. I'm
also not averse to slight changes of syntax to suit, nor even
the name of Degsy if appropriate.

The play should be performed with no set and no props, except
the chair that Greaves sits on. I would also say not to be too
concerned with getting the physical aspects of the play (eg,
driving the van) perfect, as I always intended the piece to be
'illustrative' rather than precise physical theatre.

*In the darkness, a football crowd is heard. Loud. Spotlight up
on* DEGSY.

DEGSY   It was not a goal.
                 That is all there is to understand.
                 Truth. Absolute.
                 Not a goal. No way.
                 That goal, not a goal.

                 (CLIFF, *in spotlight.*)

CLIFF   When I got in, it was early, or very late,
                 depending on how you see these things, and I
                 noticed there was a message on the machine.

DEGSY   Cliff, Cliff, Cliff . . .

CLIFF   That's me.

DEGSY   Oi, oi, where the . . . get to the phone now.
                 Now. Now.

CLIFF   It was Degsy.

DEGSY   It's Degsy. Cliff, it's Degsy.

CLIFF   As though it could have been anyone else.

DEGSY   I've done it, oh yes, oh yes, I have done it
                 Clifford, me old son.

CLIFF   I couldn't help noticing he seemed –

DEGSY   One-nil, one-nil, one-nil, one-nil to us mate!

CLIFF   A touch over excited, you know considering –

DEGSY   He's here, I've got him, I've got him sitting
                 here.

CLIFF   And he kept repeating –

DEGSY   Right here, he is sitting right here Cliff, I've
             done it, I have, only gone and fucking done it,
             oh yes, fucking hell mate, oh yes!

CLIFF   And I thought –

DEGSY   Get over here now, you have got to see this.

CLIFF   See what?

DEGSY   Get over here now. Now.

CLIFF   Eh?

DEGSY   Now.

CLIFF   So I jumped in the van, and . . . I got to
             Degsy's.

             (*Lights up.* GREAVES *sits, tied up in a chair.*
             CLIFF *stares in disbelief.*)

CLIFF   And sitting there, was, was . . . was . . .

             (CLIFF *takes in* GREAVES.)

CLIFF   . . . wh-what, what have you done?

DEGSY   I'm making a difference Cliff. I am saying,
             enough is enough.

CLIFF   What the fuck have you done?

DEGSY   Something had to be done, and I'm doing it.

CLIFF   What the fuck have you done?!

DEGSY   I have done the right thing.

CLIFF   What the fucking fuck have you done?

DEGSY   Oi, will you stop saying –

CLIFF   What the fuck have you done?

DEGSY   Cliff, I said, you are not –

CLIFF   What the fuck have you done!? What the,
               Degsy, what have you fucking done, oh Jesus,
               what have you done, I don't believe this, what
               have you done, oh fucking hell Degsy, oh fuck.

               (DEGSY *shouts over* CLIFF.)

DEGSY   Cliff, Cliff, Cliff, Cliff!

               (CLIFF *eventually shuts up.*)

DEGSY   I have done what we talked about yesterday
               after the game.

CLIFF   What?

DEGSY   Yesterday.

CLIFF   When?

DEGSY   After the game.

CLIFF   Where?

DEGSY   In the pub.

CLIFF   After the game?

DEGSY   Yes.

CLIFF   In the pub?

DEGSY   Yes.

CLIFF   But you disappeared?

DEGSY   I know, I was busy.

CLIFF   Jesus, you mean . . .

DEGSY   You said it was a great idea.

CLIFF   Did I?

DEGSY   You said it was a great idea. You said it was
             about time somebody stood up and put their
             money where their mouth was.

CLIFF   Are you sure that was me Degs, there were a
             lot of people –

DEGSY   I have witnesses, Cliff.

CLIFF   Oh look, I was in mourning for my life.

DEGSY   Exactly. And why was that?

CLIFF   But that doesn't mean . . .

DEGSY   What?

CLIFF   That doesn't mean you go out and do it!?

DEGSY   It wasn't a goal! We were cheated.

CLIFF   I know we were cheated, but –

DEGSY   Don't start with the buts.

CLIFF   But Degsy –

DEGSY   There is always a but with you. We have to see
             this through.

CLIFF   But . . . we? We?!

DEGSY   We have to grab these bastards by the short
             and curlies!

CLIFF   But Degsy –

DEGSY   No buts.

CLIFF   But Degsy –

DEGSY	I said no buts, Cliff.
CLIFF	This is the sort of thing nutters do.
	(*Beat.*)
DEGSY	So what are you saying?
CLIFF	I didn't mean that to sound like it sounded.
DEGSY	Are you saying I'm a nutter?
CLIFF	No.
DEGSY	I am not a nutter.
CLIFF	No, you're not a nutter Degsy –
DEGSY	You'd better not be about to say but again.
	(*Beat.*)
CLIFF	But Degsy . . .
DEGSY	I knew I shouldn't have rung you. I knew it. I knew it.
CLIFF	All I'm saying, is that, maybe . . .
DEGSY	All talk and no fucking bottle, that's you.
CLIFF	Maybe, just maybe Degs, but maybe, you might have over-reacted here.
DEGSY	I know, I know I have done the right thing.
CLIFF	You've kidnapped another human being.
DEGSY	Oh, what is this? You joined Amnesty International all of a sudden?
CLIFF	I'm just saying it's a bit drastic.

DEGSY   I should have just done it. Kept me head down,
            kept you out of it.

CLIFF   He's just a bloke.

DEGSY   No, no, no, sorry, he is not just a bloke.

CLIFF   Don't be daft.

DEGSY   Anyway that is so not relevant, that is so not
            the point.

CLIFF   Ok, so what is the point then?

DEGSY   The point is Cliff, I will tell you what the point
            is.

CLIFF   Yes please.

DEGSY   I'll tell you what the point is Cliff, I am going to
            tell you what the point is, because the point is
            Cliff, the point is, you know what the point is.

CLIFF   No I don't.

DEGSY   The point is Cliff, the point is, the point is . . .

CLIFF   What? What? Enlighten me. Come on Degsy,
            what is the point?

DEGSY   The point is, don't interrupt me like that, I
            cannot stand it when you fucking interrupt me!

CLIFF   Well tell me what the frigging point is then!

DEGSY   The point is Cliff . . . I have taken the man
            responsible.

            (*Beat.*)

CLIFF   So, in other words, let me clear up any
            misunderstandings I might have here, but you
            have, correct me if I'm wrong, but you have
            kidnapped the referee from yesterday's game?

	(*Beat.*)
DEGSY	Yes.
	(*Beat.*)
CLIFF	Why?
DEGSY	It was not a goal.
CLIFF	But why have you kidnapped the referee?
DEGSY	It was not a goal.
CLIFF	OK, OK, let's try a different tack here . . . why?
DEGSY	It was not a goal. Listen to me, Cliff. That goal, not a goal. Do you hear me? It was not a goal.
CLIFF	Degsy, Degsy, to us it was not a goal, to us it was a cruel twist of fate, helped, I agree, not inconsiderably by 'Exhibit A' sitting here, but, the problem is, Degs –
DEGSY	But this, but that, will you change the fucking record!
CLIFF	The problem is everyone else has actually agreed that it was a goal. Obviously a lot of people were upset, I mean, eh, our Swiss manager –
DEGSY	Our third this season.
CLIFF	He nearly got himself arrested –
DEGSY	Nearly never achieved nothing.
CLIFF	Maybe I should explain. When Degsy says our third this season he doesn't mean we've had three managers this season who all happen to to be Swiss, he means we have actually had three managers this season.

(DEGSY *complains under speech.*)

DEGSY It was not a goal. (*Repeats.*)

CLIFF Degsy, Degsy, it was a goal, we lost, we have been relegated, we have gone down, we went to the pub, we got pissed, some of us got very pissed, some of us watched it on the telly, even Barry Venison said it was a goal, admittedly a very dodgy one, but the theory that it wasn't a goal does not stand up to a great deal of scrutiny, does it?

(*Beat.*)

DEGSY No.

(*Beat.*)

CLIFF Is that a no meaning you agree with me or is that a no meaning what?

DEGSY No.

CLIFF No?

DEGSY No.

CLIFF No? What do you mean, no?

DEGSY Why is it a goal?

CLIFF Because, it is.

DEGSY Why?

CLIFF Because, we all saw it, it's in the paper. There's even a fucking pull-out spread.

DEGSY No, no, no, it doesn't have to be like that.

CLIFF What?

DEGSY   All he has to do is say it wasn't a goal.

CLIFF   Eh?

DEGSY   All he has to do is say he fucked up, he made a mistake, they have to play the game again, we win, we stay up.

CLIFF   As simple as that?

DEGSY   Yes.

CLIFF   Has anyone mentioned there might be a few flaws in your rationale here?

DEGSY   Hey, mister fucking evening class, sarcasm is easy, taking the piss, anyone can do that, but taking action, doing something about it, making a difference, that's a bit more difficult, and, and that's what I'm doing, I'm making a difference.

CLIFF   I don't believe this.

DEGSY   Hey Cliff, believe it.

             (*Beat.*)

CLIFF   You may have gathered that the team Degsy and myself follow has recently undergone a certain amount of disappointment.

DEGSY   It was not a goal. That is what all this is about.

CLIFF   We have not had a good season.

DEGSY   And we don't deserve to go down, that is fact, even Alan Hansen said we had too many good players to go down.

CLIFF   We started the season alright, not great, mid-table, chugging along –

DEGSY   Do you hear me? The original Scottish thunderbird himself said –

CLIFF   Degsy, I heard you.

DEGSY   Too many good players, that's –

CLIFF   Degsy, point made.

DEGSY   Too many good players. That's what he said.

             (*Beat.*)

CLIFF   After Christmas, we went into freefall, it was
             dire.

DEGSY   We didn't score for six games.

CLIFF   Seven if you count the League Cup.

DEGSY   I don't count that.

CLIFF   It was diabolical.

DEGSY   We were like some sort of drop-in centre for
             overpaid wankers.

CLIFF   It was not happening.

DEGSY   We were dead from the knees down.

CLIFF   Nil-nil, two-one –

DEGSY   To them.

CLIFF   Three-nil –

DEGSY   To them.

CLIFF   Two more nil-nils, a very embarrassing –

DEGSY   Fucking shameful!

CLIFF   Five-one home defeat, it was –

DEGSY   Shite!

CLIFF	Shiteloads of shite.
DEGSY	And then somehow –
CLIFF	Somehow? Do you think a complete absence of form might have had something to do with it?
DEGSY	We dropped –
CLIFF	Into the relegation zone.
DEGSY	I felt sick.
CLIFF	It was not a good feeling.
DEGSY	It was like some bad joke.
CLIFF	And the punchline was –
DEGSY	Last game of the season.
CLIFF	We need to win.
DEGSY	Depending on other results.
CLIFF	But basically we need to win. Not lose.
DEGSY	We definitely do not want to lose.
CLIFF	If we lose –
DEGSY	We are fucked.
CLIFF	Fucked big style.
	(*Beat.*)
CLIFF	So, eighty-fourth minute.
DEGSY	Nil-nil.
CLIFF	Piss-poor match, but it stays like this, and we are staying up. Just.

DEGSY	Corner to us. That blonde Scandinavian bollocks takes it.
CLIFF	Amazingly it doesn't go straight to the head of a defender.
DEGSY	It hangs towards the back post.
CLIFF	Their goalie is up for it.
DEGSY	But our number twenty-three –
CLIFF	Brick shithouse as he is lovingly known.
DEGSY	He's up there.
CLIFF	Their goalie gets his hands to it, but that's all, and it slips free.
DEGSY	And then before we know it . . .
CLIFF	It's in the net.
DEGSY	It came off his shoulder.
CLIFF	Mister brick shithouse has scored.
DEGSY	Off his shoulder.
CLIFF	In the fucking net.
DEGSY	Their defence is complaining about something, but hey what's new.
CLIFF	Our end has gone bananas!
DEGSY	It is beautiful!
CLIFF	Mayhem!
DEGSY	The pain in my chest I've been walking round with all season, it's gone.

CLIFF	One-nil.
DEGSY	To us.
CLIFF	The scoreboard's flashing.
DEGSY	Even the frigging mascot –
CLIFF	A giant squirrel, don't ask why –
DEGSY	Is on the pitch –
CLIFF	And most of our team is having an orgy down by the corner-flag.
DEGSY	We are staying up.
CLIFF	But –
DEGSY	Eh?
CLIFF	What?
DEGSY	No!?
CLIFF	The ref has blown.
DEGSY	He's what?
CLIFF	The ref has blown for something.
DEGSY	I do not fucking believe it!?
CLIFF	It's not a goal.
DEGSY	Of course it's a goal, it went in the net!
CLIFF	The scoreboard stops flashing.
DEGSY	And then –
CLIFF	They've taken a free-kick –
DEGSY	Oi, they can't do that!

CLIFF	They've taken a free kick and there's three of the bastards running towards our goal.
DEGSY	Seriously fucking legging it.
CLIFF	And where, oi, where's our defence?!
DEGSY	Down by the corner-flag with their tongues down each others throats!
CLIFF	Three against one –
DEGSY	Oh, and eventually –
CLIFF	The party breaks up –
DEGSY	And –
CLIFF	The look on their faces –
DEGSY	Three against one.
CLIFF	When they realise that we are in deep shit here.
DEGSY	Very deep shit.
CLIFF	Very very deep shit.
DEGSY	The deepest shit imaginable.
	(*They wince. The goal is scored.*)
CLIFF	Our goalie gets a fingertip to it.
DEGSY	If there is one thing football has taught me, never trust a goalie with dyed-orange hair.
CLIFF	And for one moment I think this cannot be.
DEGSY	This is not right.
CLIFF	This is not happening.

DEGSY	But it is.
CLIFF	It has happened.
DEGSY	One-nil.
CLIFF	To them.
DEGSY	Not us.
CLIFF	One-fucking-nil.
DEGSY	To them.

(*Beat.*)

DEGSY   We are going down.

(*Silence. The figure tied to the chair makes a noise. They turn to look at him.*)

CLIFF   Are you sure it's him?

DEGSY   Of course I'm sure. What do you take me for?

CLIFF   I thought he had more hair than that.

DEGSY   It's him. Antony bastard Greaves. The wanker who has ruined our lives.

CLIFF   I'm just saying –

DEGSY   What? You're just saying what?

CLIFF   I'm just saying he looks a bit different close-up.

DEGSY   Everyone looks a bit different close-up.

CLIFF   I'm just saying you might have made a mistake.

DEGSY   I have not made a mistake.

CLIFF   But you might have?

DEGSY   I have not made a mistake.

CLIFF   Well, how did you find him?

DEGSY   I looked him up in the phone book.

CLIFF   What?

DEGSY   Watch my lips, I looked him up –

CLIFF   In the phone book, oh yes, the foolproof
             masterplan.

DEGSY   I'm warning you.

CLIFF   You looked him up in the phone book? You
             looked him up –

DEGSY   Hey, it's him. It's him alright.

CLIFF   Degsy's home these days was, how shall I put
             it, radically minimal. Things seemed to not be
             there any more. But he still had a telly, and he
             had the game on video. The highlights, not that
             there were many. But he had the eighty-fourth
             minute. The corner. The goal. The false
             celebration. The free-kick. The sheer panic. The
             goalkeepers fingertips. The deafening silence.
             And then the close up of a ref surrounded by
             the hopeless helpless protestations of a team
             who know they are fucked. Oh yes, it was him
             alright. Degsy even froze the picture. It was
             him.

             (GREAVES *makes a sound.*)

CLIFF   I think he wants to say something.

             (CLIFF *looks at* DEGSY. DEGSY *indicates for*
             CLIFF *to take the gag off. Silence.*)

DEGSY   Go on then, we're all waiting.

(GREAVES *talks directly to the audience.*)

GREAVES   I was thinking of going to bed when, when I heard something. I live on my own these days, not that that's relevant, and anyway, it was the sort of sound, a human sound, not speech, but movement, something like a footstep.

DEGSY   He lived in one of those places with a driveway and hedges between the houses.

GREAVES   And I thought that's strange . . .

DEGSY   And the back door was open. I mean, what do you expect if you go round leaving your back door open?

GREAVES   I thought that's not right somehow. And then there was a bigger sound, a more definite sound. Like . . . like someone falling over.

DEGSY   It was dark. Strange house.

GREAVES   And I went to see what it was. I don't think I really thought it was someone, it all happened so quickly, and then –

DEGSY   We were looking at each other.

GREAVES   A chill ran down my spine.

DEGSY   You're coming with me!

GREAVES   He said.

CLIFF   I do not believe you looked him up in the phone book!

GREAVES   I couldn't see his face very clearly. It was very shadowy. And I could see he was holding something. And I thought, he's got a gun.

(CLIFF *is disturbed by this piece of information.*)

DEGSY   Did you hear me, you're coming with me.

GREAVES   He said again.

CLIFF   A gun? Where did you get a gun from? What
               are you doing with a gun?

DEGSY   It wasn't a gun.

CLIFF   But he said –

DEGSY   He thought I had a gun!

GREAVES   It was a cricket bat. It wasn't a gun, it was a
               cricket bat. I could see that when he moved
               towards me.

CLIFF   What are you doing with a cricket bat? You've
               always hated cricket.

DEGSY   It is not important where I got a cricket bat
               from.

CLIFF   And how does a cricket bat look like a gun? I
               mean, that is one very strange gun.

GREAVES   And he held the cricket bat up to my face.
               Close. I could see his eyes.

DEGSY   And do you know what? He was wearing
               glasses. The bastard had a pair of bifocals
               perched on the end of his nose.

GREAVES   I only wear them for reading.

DEGSY   Can you friggin' believe that?

CLIFF   What?

DEGSY   He was wearing glasses.

CLIFF   Oh right, got you. Ref. Glasses. Ironic.

GREAVES	I could smell his breath.
DEGSY	And he was sweating. Buckets. It was dribbling off the end of his chin.
GREAVES	And I could almost feel him thinking –
DEGSY	Got this far, what next? I'll just hit him, show him I mean business. Show him who's boss.
GREAVES	And I thought if I can just get into the street, if I can just make it out, someone will see us, someone will call the police.
DEGSY	And then he makes a break for it.
GREAVES	Someone will be bound to see us.
DEGSY	And he's going for the front door. He's making a run for it.
CLIFF	Don't let him get away.
DEGSY	What?
CLIFF	He gets into the street, someone'll see him, they'll call the police, you've had it.
DEGSY	Well I know that, don't I?
CLIFF	Get him then.
DEGSY	I'm getting him, alright!!
GREAVES	I've got a good few yards on him.
DEGSY	But this hallway, I don't know what's what, and for a moment I can't actually see him.
GREAVES	And then –
DEGSY	There's this thud –
GREAVES	Smack!

DEGSY	The guy has run into something.
GREAVES	I've just had a new inside door put in.
DEGSY	Full on.
GREAVES	And I always keep it shut at night.
DEGSY	And I can see him toppling backwards.
GREAVES	And I black out.
DEGSY	He's out cold. The bastard has knocked himself out.
GREAVES	And the next thing I know –
DEGSY	He's done the job for me.
GREAVES	I'm lying on the back seat of a car, tied up, with a bruise that feels the size of a small county.
CLIFF	He knocked himself out!?
DEGSY	Flat out.
GREAVES	And then he brought me to this room.
DEGSY	And I tied the bastard up.
GREAVES	This room that, that feels a million miles from anywhere.

(CLIFF *puts the gag back on* GREAVES.)

DEGSY	OK, look after him.
CLIFF	What?
DEGSY	I have a phone call to make.
CLIFF	Hey, oi, what's wrong with your phone?

DEGSY	They'll trace it.
CLIFF	Degsy, please, I really don't think –
DEGSY	He's tied up, he won't do anything.
CLIFF	I haven't done this sort of thing before.
DEGSY	Cliff, you'd better not be thinking that you're . . .
CLIFF	I'll tell you what, I'll come back later.
DEGSY	Because this was all your idea.
CLIFF	Things to do, you know how it is, what do you mean it was my idea?
DEGSY	You're the brains behind this.
CLIFF	The brains? What are you on about? I've got three GCSEs and half an NVQ.
DEGSY	You're up to your neck, mate.
CLIFF	No, no, no, no, you phoned me up and –
DEGSY	I was simply following orders.
CLIFF	I am out of here. You can't lay this on me.
DEGSY	Oh yea?
CLIFF	Yea.
DEGSY	You are really going walk out on me?
CLIFF	You are taking the piss, I'm going, I'm out of here.
DEGSY	I heard you the first time.

CLIFF   I cannot handle this, I am off, I am exit-bound, no offence mate, but honestly count me out, arrivederci, so long, farewell, ta-ra!

DEGSY   Go on then.

CLIFF   What?

DEGSY   Go.

CLIFF   I am going, I don't know if you noticed, but that's what I'm doing.

DEGSY   If you're going, go.

CLIFF   I am, I'm just saying –

DEGSY   Go.

(*Beat.*)

CLIFF   I know you Degsy, you're just using reverse psychology.

DEGSY   What are you on about now?

CLIFF   You think you'll get me to stay by making out you're not bothered if I go.

DEGSY   Cliff, the door is that way.

CLIFF   See, you're doing it now.

DEGSY   Cliff, fuck off.

CLIFF   You think I'm going to think you want me to fuck off but really –

DEGSY   No really, Cliff, fuck off.

CLIFF   But really, Degsy –

DEGSY   But really, Cliff –

CLIFF	. . . but really, Degsy, you need me.
DEGSY	OK, stay then.
CLIFF	Ah-ha.
DEGSY	What?
CLIFF	Now you're going for double reverse psychology.
DEGSY	Oh, for fu . . .
CLIFF	You're making out you're not bothered whether I stay or go, but really . . .
DEGSY	I thought you were going.
CLIFF	I am. I'm just saying . . .
DEGSY	Well toodle-fucking-pip then.

(*Beat.*)

CLIFF	You think I'm not going to go, don't you?

(CLIFF *goes to exit, turns back.*)

CLIFF	You think I haven't got the bottle to just walk out, to just think, fuck Degsy, let him sort this one out on his own.

(CLIFF *goes to exit, turns back.*)

CLIFF	You think, oh yea Cliff, we all know what Cliff's like, we all know Cliff the sap, Cliff the sidekick, Cliff, Degsy's mate, he'll go along with whatever mad fucking thing you've done this time, and hey, do you notice, it's always Cliff, Degsy's mate, never Degsy, Cliff's mate, oh no, always, hey, it's Cliff, Degsy's mate, hello Cliff, you're Degsy's mate aren't you, that's me, Cliff, Degsy's mate, Cliff, Degsy's mate. Sometimes I think it's like me fucking surname.

DEGSY	I thought you were going.
	(*Beat.*)
CLIFF	I am.
	(CLIFF *exits.*)
DEGSY	(*to* GREAVES) He hasn't gone. He's just . . . he hasn't gone anywhere.
	(*Beat.*)
DEGSY	Alright Cliff, come on.
	(*An awkward tension.*)
DEGSY	Cliff?!
	(*Beat.*)
DEGSY	Cliff!!?!
	(*Beat.*)
DEGSY	The frigging soft knobhead, and I think, I am going to have him for this, because this is petty, this is piss-taking super-league, and so I storm into the hallway, and, and, he's not there, he has actually, the door is wide open, and the cheeky bastard has done a runner, and I'm standing there, and I think, and I remember, and I think, at least, at least she slammed the door, at least she knew how to make an exit, at least, fucking drama queen, and I remembered thinking, standing there like a wet prick, thinking, oh yea, very good, nice one, very dramatic and all that but she'll be back, she'll come home with her suitcase between her legs, no matter what, no matter how badly you say I behave, she'll be back. Oh yes, she'll be back. Oh yes, on my life, she'll be back, she won't mean it this time, oh yes, she will be back.

(*Music. 'There She Goes' by The La's.* DEGSY *walks away, devastated.* CLIFF *re-enters. He signals for the music to be cut just before the vocals start.* DEGSY *turns, half-hoping it might be the woman who walked out on him. It isn't.*)

DEGSY   Missing me already, were you?

CLIFF   You mad bastard.

DEGSY   You mad bastard's mate.

             (*Beat.*)

CLIFF   Eventually, it was decided, after some discussion.

DEGSY   I'm off to make that fucking phone call, you stay here.

CLIFF   That I would stay with Greaves.

             (DEGSY *exits.* CLIFF *moves around the room, trying to look threatening.*)

CLIFF   Conversation was . . .

             (*Beat.*)

CLIFF   Awkward.

             (*Beat.*)

CLIFF   Don't start thinking we're going to get friendly or anything? I know the scenario. We find some common bond, kidnapper and kidnapee, you know, we begin to understand each other, all that shit, oh no, definitely no, no way, not today.

             (*Beat.*)

CLIFF   I'm just saying, that is not going to happen.

(*Beat.*)

CLIFF   I'm not going to ask you what it's like being a ref, or anything like that. What it's like before a big game, do you feel nervous, the tension, the dressing room banter with the linesmen, none of that. No, don't want to know.

(*Beat.*)

CLIFF   How do you get on with the players? None of that.

(*Beat.*)

CLIFF   No, no thank you, no. No, no, no.

(*Beat.* DEGSY *enters.*)

DEGSY   I phoned up a local radio phone-in.

CLIFF   He disguised his voice.

DEGSY   Apparently they thought it was a wind-up at first.

CLIFF   Sounded sort of gruff American.

DEGSY   But then they did a bit of research.

CLIFF   A bit like Bruce Willis in 'Armageddon'.

DEGSY   And they soon found out this was no joke.

(*Beat.*)

CLIFF   It was on all the lunchtime news programmes.

(*Beat.*)

CLIFF   And it was just after that that Degsy started playing the video.

DEGSY   Repeat after me, he is not fouling the goalie, it is a goal.

CLIFF   And Greaves just sat there.

DEGSY   That is a goal, the other isn't. That is a goal, the –

CLIFF   Not that he could actually go very far.

DEGSY   Why don't we just watch it again?

CLIFF   And we did. We watched it again.

DEGSY   Tell me, how is that not a goal?

CLIFF   And then we watched it again.

DEGSY   Jesus, he is nowhere near the goalie!

CLIFF   And we watched it again after that.

DEGSY   Oi!

CLIFF   And once again after that.

DEGSY   Oi, you!

CLIFF   And Greaves still just sat there.

DEGSY   Oi, Greaves!

CLIFF   Didn't say a word.

DEGSY   Oi, Greaves – what have you got to say for yourself?

                 (GREAVES *indicates that he would like to say something.*)

CLIFF   Hey Degsy, I think he wants to –

DEGSY   Take it off.

(Cliff *removes the gag.* Degsy *stares.* Greaves *stares back.*)

DEGSY   Come on then.

GREAVES   You really are a very deluded individual.

DEGSY   You what?

GREAVES   If you think terrorism is an answer.

DEGSY   Terrorism? What are you on about?

GREAVES   You can't get your way, so you resort to violence.

DEGSY   You made a wrong decision, therefore –

GREAVES   No I didn't.

DEGSY   Yes you did.

GREAVES   No I didn't.

DEGSY   Yes you did!

GREAVES   No I didn't!

DEGSY   Yes you did, yes you did, yes you did, you did, you did, you did, yes you did, yes you did!

GREAVES   You are unhinged.

DEGSY   Well, someone has to be.

GREAVES   He was interfering with the goalkeeper.

DEGSY   Inter . . . interfering? Hey he's not some dirty old pervert like you.

GREAVES   I stand by my decision.

DEGSY   Do you?

GREAVES   And whatever you might say the opposing team were given adequate time to regroup after the decision.

DEGSY   You've got a nerve, calling me deluded.

GREAVES   Your team lost, there is nothing you can do about it.

DEGSY   Hey, just you wait and see.

GREAVES   This is pathetic.

DEGSY   Fascist.

GREAVES   Oh a fascist, am I?

DEGSY   Yea, because if I'm a terrorist –

GREAVES   Of course, me and Hitler, what an astute comparison –

DEGSY   Because if I'm a terrorist –

GREAVES   No, I'm sorry about that, you're actually a moron –

DEGSY   I am not a moron!

GREAVES   Actually I think you might be.

DEGSY   I, I am the voice, I am the voice –

GREAVES   A moronic thug.

DEGSY   Of the, the fucking masses, mate. I am speaking up for all those who, who . . . who . . .

CLIFF   Don't speak up.

DEGSY   Exactly. That's me, that is.

GREAVES   Is it?

DEGSY	There are a plenty of people out there who want to do what I'm doing. Millions.
GREAVES	Millions?
DEGSY	Yea, fucking loads of millions.
GREAVES	Goodness me, that is a lot.
DEGSY	Yea, you living there in your poncy house with your double-glazing and all that shite, you haven't got a clue about what, what's happening out here, down on the streets.
GREAVES	So where are they, then?
DEGSY	Eh?
GREAVES	The great unwashed. Where are they?
DEGSY	Are you taking the piss?
GREAVES	Shouldn't they be putting up the barricades as we speak?
DEGSY	Hey, don't you fucking worry mate, they're out there, and when they hear what I've done, they'll, they'll do something, oh yea, they'll back me up big time, oh yes, won't they Cliff?

(CLIFF *has drifted off during this exchange.*)

DEGSY	Cliff?
CLIFF	What?
DEGSY	Won't they?
CLIFF	Oh yea.
DEGSY	You weren't fucking listening.
CLIFF	Yes I was.

DEGSY	I don't believe you sometimes.
CLIFF	(*to audience*) I'd only drifted off for a few seconds.
DEGSY	Here I am trying to –
CLIFF	I was thinking how I really did not want to see that bit of video again.
DEGSY	Cliff!?
CLIFF	What?
DEGSY	You're doing it again.
CLIFF	What's that?

(*Beat.*)

DEGSY   Put his gag back on.

(CLIFF *puts* GREAVES' *gag back on him.*)

CLIFF   And Degsy did play the video again. And again. The same few minutes. The corner. The disallowed goal. The other goal. The close-up of Greaves as he tries to restart the game. The same few minutes. Again and again. He stood there with the remote control, rewinding, playing, stopping, rewinding, playing, stopping. Ten times, twenty times, when it got to over thirty, forty, it was like, I felt, I remember thinking, we were in a very, very strange area of the human psyche here. And Greaves just sat there. He reminded me of Alec Guinness in *The Bridge On the River Kwai*. It was like that, it was, like some sort of weird Japanese torture, sixty, seventy, no let up, the same mad bit of football, over and over, the noises, the crowd, the commentator, it became like this music, and sometimes I thought, it won't be the same this time, it can't possibly just repeat itself, the video will get bored, it'll change the ending, our goal will stand, there'll be a streaker, anything, anything just to fucking stop it repeating itself, and Greaves, he just sat there, it must have been ninety times through, over a hundred, Jesus I don't know, because my head was beginning to throb badly, very badly, badly throbbing badly, and I'm thinking 'Degsy will you give over'.

DEGSY   Oi, watch the video.

CLIFF   How long you going to keep this up?

DEGSY   As long as it takes.

CLIFF   As long as it takes? And when Degsy said that, I don't know, my head, it said Cliff, Clifford, you have had enough, and there, right next to my foot was a cricket bat, presumably the cricket bat-come-gun from previous, and I picked it up, I picked it up by its rubber handle, and I went for that fucking telly, I went for it, I fucking laid into it like some mad avenging nemesis come to kill all who stood in its way, and I went through that screen with a pleasure only known to true vandals, and it smashed beautifully, easily, and there was a bit of smoke, and the sound of electricity having a really hard time, and then I pushed it, I pushed it hard so it rolled off its perch and smashed to the floor, and I whacked it again, and kicked it, and let it know who it was dealing with, and I kept it up, cricket bat, foot, cricket bat, foot, and then finally I picked it up, and I lifted it above my head, and I held it there for a moment, for dramatic effect, and then I just let it drop, I let gravity do its work, and I watched as it smashed, cracked and splintered open like the useless piece of old crap it was.

                         (*Pause.* CLIFF *begins to regain his senses.*)

DEGSY   Cliff?

CLIFF	I had seriously lost it.
DEGSY	Cliff?
	(*Pause.*)
CLIFF	Sorry.
DEGSY	What?
CLIFF	Sorry. I . . . I lost it, I don't know what happened.
DEGSY	You lost it?
CLIFF	Yea, my head, it went funny.
DEGSY	That was my telly, Cliff.
CLIFF	That's never happened to me before.
DEGSY	What am I going to watch now, Cliff?
CLIFF	What?
DEGSY	You have committed armageddon upon my television, Cliff.
CLIFF	I'm sorry, Degsy.
DEGSY	I don't want sorry, I want my television back.
CLIFF	I'm really sorry, I just couldn't take it any more. It just sort of happened.
	(GREAVES *has started laughing through his gag. They turn to look at him.*)
DEGSY	Is he laughing?
	(*He stares for a moment.*)
DEGSY	Take his gag off.

CLIFF   Why?

DEGSY   Take his gag off.

(CLIFF *takes his gag off.*)

DEGSY   Are you laughing?

(GREAVES *can't help himself and bursts out laughing again.*)

DEGSY   Are you laughing at us?

(*He keeps on laughing, despite himself.*)

DEGSY   Greaves? Are you laughing at us?

CLIFF   I don't think he was Degsy, sounded like he had something caught in his throat.

DEGSY   Shut up. Oi, Greaves – are you laughing at us?

CLIFF   Now Degsy is not a violent man.

DEGSY   You fucking laugh at us again and I'll break both your legs!

CLIFF   Honestly, it's just sometimes he gets a bit carried away.

DEGSY   And I'll take that pea out of your whistle and shove it so far up your arse –

CLIFF   I think they've moved on from peas in whistles, Degs.

DEGSY   Shut up.

CLIFF   And then, before I knew it, he hit him.

(*Slap.*)

CLIFF   He hit him. He slapped him. Not as hard as he could have, but, still, he did it, and it was like,

when someone hits someone else, it's not like
on the telly or in a film, it's like, it's more real if
you know what I mean.

DEGSY   That is a warning.

CLIFF   Degsy!?

DEGSY   Consider that a yellow fucking card.

CLIFF   What did you do that for?

DEGSY   He was laughing, he was taking the piss.

CLIFF   Don't hit him Degs, that's not wise.

DEGSY   Not wise? Not wise? That's a bit rich coming
             from the bastard offspring of Keith Moon and
             the Incredible Hulk.

CLIFF   But you don't have to hit him?

DEGSY   How am I going to break him down? Eh? How
             am I going to break him down without a telly? I
             was just getting going, and you fucking
             destroyed it.

             (GREAVES *starts to repeat the following.*
             Quietly at first, getting louder.)

GREAVES   (*under breath*) Forgive them Lord, they know
             not what they do.

DEGSY   You fucking trashed it.

CLIFF   Don't look at me like that, Degs.

DEGSY   Like what?

CLIFF   Like you want to kill me.

DEGSY   But I do want to kill you.

(DEGSY *and* CLIFF *register* GREAVES *is saying something.*)

GREAVES   Forgive them Lord, they know not what they do.

             (*Pause.*)

DEGSY   What's going on? What's he doing?

GREAVES   (*repeats*) Forgive them Lord, they know not what they do.

DEGSY   Oi, oi, oi!

             (DEGSY *and* CLIFF *are in a panic as to what is going on.*)

DEGSY   What are you doing?

             (GREAVES *keeps repeating his phrase.*)

DEGSY   I said, what are you doing?

CLIFF   He seems to be forgiving us.

DEGSY   Forgiving us?

CLIFF   Yes.

DEGSY   That is, what? Forgiving us? This is a bit fucking weird. I don't like this. I don't like this at all.

CLIFF   He's obviously a bit religious.

DEGSY   What?

CLIFF   You know, religious – Jesus on the cross, Catholic, Pope, kissing tarmacs . . .

DEGSY   Religious?

CLIFF   Turning the other cheek, all that. Forgiveness.

DEGSY   You mean . . .

GREAVES   You will not shake my faith.

DEGSY   You mean I can hit him as much as I like and
             he'll still forgive me?

CLIFF   I don't think that's what he means.

DEGSY   A football ref who happens to be a Christian?
             Jesus, what a combination.

GREAVES   Good will triumph.

DEGSY   Good will triumph, eh? Only if there's a decent
             ref.

CLIFF   Degsy . . .

DEGSY   Hey, if he forgives me whatever I happen to do,
             that gives me a lot of possibilities.

CLIFF   Degsy . . .

GREAVES   I may forgive you now, but remember that
             ultimately you will have to face –

DEGSY   Shut up.

CLIFF   Don't.

DEGSY   Don't what?

CLIFF   Don't, do, whatever it is you're thinking of
             doing.

             (*Silence.*)

CLIFF   And Degsy started moving towards Greaves.
             Dead slow.

GREAVES   I prepared myself.

CLIFF	It was like he was toying with him.
	(*Beat.*)
CLIFF	And then . . .
	(DEGSY *is very close to* GREAVES.)
CLIFF	The phone rang.
DEGSY	Fucking hell! Who's that?
CLIFF	It's the phone, Degs.
DEGSY	I know it's the phone, I know a phone when I hear one.
CLIFF	Shall I get it?
DEGSY	No.
	(*They look at the phone.*)
CLIFF	And it kept on ringing.
	(*They carry on looking at the phone.*)
CLIFF	Whoever it was, they weren't giving up.
	(*They carry on looking at the phone.*)
CLIFF	It was the most determined phone ring I've ever heard in my life.
	(*Still they carry on looking at the phone.*)
CLIFF	Hey we'd better answer it.
DEGSY	Why?
CLIFF	They might come round.
DEGSY	What?

CLIFF	They might think, oh I'll pop round, Degsy's not in, I'll pop round with something, say hello in person sort of thing, maybe drop a note through the door, and as they're dropping the note through the door, they notice something untoward, like, like, something amiss, something not quite right, and they might mention it to someone else, and somehow, before you know it, they've called the police, and the police, they'll come round, and they'll think, hello what's happening here, I'll just sledgehammer the door down, and then –

(DEGSY *moves to phone.*)

CLIFF	Degsy picked up the phone.
DEGSY	Yea, who is it?
CLIFF	And I could tell who it was straightaway.
DEGSY	What? Where are you?
CLIFF	He didn't say her name, but there was only one person it could be. She was obviously doing most of the talking, and then he said –
DEGSY	What? Now? You can't come round now. No, yes, I know you've got a key, no, no, you can't come round, did you hear me, you can't come round –
CLIFF	I think she wanted to come round.
DEGSY	No. No, that is not possible, that is not –

(*Beat.*)

CLIFF	She hung up. Degsy went quiet. He went very quiet.

(*Silence.*)

CLIFF	Was that Phillippa, Degs?

(*Silence.*)

CLIFF   Degs? Was that, er, Phillippa on the phone?

DEGSY   Yea.

CLIFF   Is she, is she popping round, is she?

DEGSY   Yea.

CLIFF   When, when might that be then?

(*Silence.*)

CLIFF   Degs? When is, is that, er, when, you just say Degs, and I'll scoot off for a bit, you, you just say.

DEGSY   Imminent, Cliff. Very fucking imminent.

CLIFF   Oh, quite soon then.

DEGSY   And do you know why she's coming round, Cliff?

(DEGSY *stares at* CLIFF.)

CLIFF   Er, well, I could have a guess I suppose . . .

DEGSY   She's coming round to pick up a few remaining possessions.

CLIFF   Is she?

DEGSY   And do you know what one of those possessions would happen to be?

CLIFF   Er . . .

DEGSY   Go on have a guess. Have a stab in the dark. What would be an ironic twist to the story thus far?

CLIFF   Is it the television, Degs?

DEGSY   No, it's the toilet seat, of course it's the
             fucking television!

             (DEGSY *is very frustrated.*)

CLIFF   That's not your television then? I always
             thought that was your television. Well, I
             thought it was a joint television, I suppose. I
             didn't realise that it was just Phillippa's. Not
             the sort of thing you think about normally, is
             it? Why should you? I mean –

DEGSY   Shut it.

CLIFF   I shut it.

DEGSY   What are we going to do?

CLIFF   I was thinking that.

DEGSY   Any ideas?

CLIFF   Not many.

DEGSY   How many is not many?

CLIFF   None.

DEGSY   (*idea*) Have you got your van?

CLIFF   Yes. No.

DEGSY   How did you get here then?

CLIFF   I walked, I ran, yea, jogged all the way.

DEGSY   It's there, I can see it out the fucking window.

CLIFF   Not the van Degs, keep the van out of it.

DEGSY   Give me the keys.

CLIFF	You're not insured. I can't just give you the keys.
DEGSY	You drive then.
CLIFF	I don't drive well under pressure, you know that, anyway, what's wrong with your car?
DEGSY	It's knackered. People'll notice it.
CLIFF	What if people notice my van? It's got my name and phone number all over it.
DEGSY	Come on, untie him.
CLIFF	Degsy, Degsy, honestly, the carburetor's fucked.
DEGSY	We'll go to your place.
CLIFF	It's making this really dodgy noise.
	(CLIFF *does an impression of dodgy noise.*)
DEGSY	We can hole up there.
CLIFF	More than two people and it starts groaning, what?
DEGSY	Come on, shift.
CLIFF	My place?
DEGSY	Yea.
CLIFF	What? Take him to my place? My place? My flat?
DEGSY	Yea.
CLIFF	No.
DEGSY	Let's go.

CLIFF   No, no, look, the central heating, it's, it's very tempremental at the moment, freezing, brass fucking monkeys –

DEGSY   Let's go.

CLIFF   But, but, what about the neighbours?

DEGSY   The neighbours? You mean that doped-up technohead and the old dear who walks round town with a stethoscope?

CLIFF   Yea, they might notice something.

DEGSY   Oh yea and my other car's a jag.

CLIFF   But Degsy –

DEGSY   Let's go.

            (*Beat.*)

CLIFF   We found a bin-bag, and shoved it over his head.

DEGSY   He struggled a bit, but –

CLIFF   He seemed sort of resigned.

DEGSY   And we threw him in the back of the van.

CLIFF   He knocked his head on the way in –

DEGSY   But he wasn't complaining.

CLIFF   And there was no one about.

DEGSY   There never is in my street. They're all too fucking depressed to step out their front doors.

CLIFF   And we set off.

DEGSY   Take it easy, don't do anything weird.

CLIFF	My heart was pounding, smacking against my rib-cage.
DEGSY	Left here, left here . . .
CLIFF	And there's a history of dodgy hearts in my family.
DEGSY	And go right down to the bottom . . .
CLIFF	My dad's brother-in-law, he keeled over, day before his forty-fifth birthday.
DEGSY	And round the back of the old bingo hall . . .
CLIFF	Degsy –
DEGSY	Down to the bottom and . . .
CLIFF	Degsy, I know the way to my own flat.
DEGSY	Yea but I know you, you always go the fucking scenic route.
CLIFF	Believe me, it would be fairly fucking difficult to go the scenic route round here.
DEGSY	Like that time we went to Devon and you wanted to go to that ruin.
CLIFF	Ruin? That was Stonehenge.
DEGSY	Straight down here . . . Jesus, that was dull.
CLIFF	Dull? That was not dull, that was, that was Stonehenge.
DEGSY	Oi, watch that car.
CLIFF	I am watching it.
DEGSY	And you bought a fucking tea-towel, didn't you?

CLIFF	Jesus, if I've heard it once –
DEGSY	What sort of bloke goes on holiday and buys a tea-towel? Look there's lights coming up.
CLIFF	I can see them.
DEGSY	Slow it down then.
CLIFF	I suppose you never use tea-towels, do you?
DEGSY	No I fucking don't, will you slow down, and if I did, I definitely wouldn't buy them on holiday, oi, are you stopping?
CLIFF	No I thought I'd ram this motor, overturn the van in a spectacular somersault, thus causing maximum carnage and attention.
DEGSY	Sometimes I can't help feeling you get a bit too mouthy for your own good.

(*Beat.*)

CLIFF	And my heart is now in serious hyper-drive.
DEGSY	And then I notice some fellar waving at us.
CLIFF	And when I say serious I mean fucking serious.
DEGSY	But, he's actually waving at, oi, Cliff . . .
CLIFF	What?
DEGSY	There's some fellar shouting at you over there.
CLIFF	What? Oh christ, it's Brickie.
DEGSY	Who the fuck is Brickie?
CLIFF	He's a fellar, he's a brickie.
DEGSY	Is he? Now that has to be one of the great nicknames of all time.

CLIFF	Alright, mate?
DEGSY	Don't talk to him.
CLIFF	I know, what a fucking ref, eh? What? What's that? He's been what? Some people, eh?
DEGSY	Let's go. Lights are changing, lights are changing, lights are changing.
CLIFF	Got to go Brick, er, me mate's got to go to hospital.
DEGSY	It's green, lights are green, lights are green.
CLIFF	No, nothing serious, just a check-up. Apparently it's his knees, they're too close together, yea, when he runs, they make this strange clicking sound.
DEGSY	What are you on about?
CLIFF	I don't know Degs, I'm just talking shite.
DEGSY	Hang a right here, hang a right.
CLIFF	So I hung a right, but it's a one-way.
DEGSY	It's a one-way.
CLIFF	You said hang a right.
DEGSY	But not down a one-way.
CLIFF	And cars are hooting at us. Get out of it.
DEGSY	Take a left here.
CLIFF	You said hang a right, so I hung one.
DEGSY	Take a left.
CLIFF	No.

DEGSY   Take a left, get out of here.

CLIFF   But if I take a left –

DEGSY   Take a left.

CLIFF   If I take a left we'll have to go on the motorway.

(*Beat.*)

DEGSY   What's this? We don't want to go on the motorway.

CLIFF   You said take a left.

DEGSY   Not if it means going on the motorway.

CLIFF   You said take a left, so I took a left.

DEGSY   Turn it round.

CLIFF   What?

DEGSY   Turn round.

CLIFF   We are now on a dual carriageway if you don't mind, by the way.

DEGSY   Just do a u-turn.

CLIFF   And the motorway is coming up.

DEGSY   Look cut across this bit with the trees.

CLIFF   I'm not doing that.

DEGSY   We do not want to go on the motorway. Cliff, Cliff, we don't want to go on the motorway.

(*Beat.*)

DEGSY	I said we don't want to go on the motorway. I said, Cliff, I said, are you listening to me? I said ...
	(Beat.)
DEGSY	Come off at the first exit.
CLIFF	And I'm thinking I could do with a cup of tea.
DEGSY	No.
CLIFF	There's a service station not far, oh yea, a cup of tea, a steak and kidney special and a waffle.
DEGSY	No.
CLIFF	What?
DEGSY	We are not stopping for a cup of tea or anything else.
CLIFF	How did you know that –
DEGSY	I told you Cliff, I know you. Come off at the first exit.
CLIFF	We came off at the first exit.
DEGSY	Will you look where you're going.
CLIFF	I am looking where I'm going.
DEGSY	Well look where you're going a bit better.
CLIFF	And we are in the middle of, I don't know where.
DEGSY	Where is this? Cliff, turn round.
CLIFF	There are fields and trees.
DEGSY	Keep your eyes on the road.

CLIFF	And I do not know where this is.
DEGSY	It looks like fucking hillbilly country.
CLIFF	Trees and fields? Ten minutes from where I live?
DEGSY	Turn it round.
CLIFF	I never knew that.
DEGSY	Here, go down there, Cliff.
CLIFF	What?
DEGSY	Let's get out of here.
CLIFF	And there's a fork in the road.
DEGSY	Go down there.
CLIFF	Go down where?
DEGSY	I said, Cliff, go down there.
CLIFF	And then . . .
DEGSY	Jesus, what!
CLIFF	Something darts across the road.
DEGSY	What are you doing?
CLIFF	It's a cat.
DEGSY	What?
CLIFF	It's a cat.
DEGSY	What are you –
CLIFF	I am not running over a cat.
DEGSY	Stay on the, fuck me!

CLIFF   I couldn't live with myself.

DEGSY   Cliff!

     (*Everything slows down.*)

GREAVES   It was about now that I knew we were going to crash.

CLIFF   It was a sort of slow skid.

DEGSY   A sort of slow, "fuck me, what's next?"

CLIFF   Sort of feeling.

GREAVES   Everything went quiet.

CLIFF   For a moment.

DEGSY   A missed heartbeat sort of moment.

CLIFF   Don't talk to me about missed heartbeats.

GREAVES   And I could feel us descending.

CLIFF   We came off the side of the road.

GREAVES   Nosediving.

DEGSY   I knew I should have driven.

CLIFF   Into a ditch.

GREAVES   And I managed to wedge myself in between what I think was a tyre and what felt like an old sofa.

DEGSY   Fucking hell's teeth.

GREAVES   And then there was a crunch.

CLIFF   A crash crunch.

DEGSY	A tree.
CLIFF	Not a big tree.
DEGSY	But big enough.
CLIFF	Big enough to do serious fucking damage to my van.

(Everyone screams. Silence.)

DEGSY	You twat . . .
CLIFF	Said Degsy.
DEGSY	You fucking soft arsehole.
CLIFF	After some consideration of our situation.
DEGSY	You have fucking done us, Cliff.
CLIFF	My van?
DEGSY	You have really fucking blown it.
CLIFF	What about my van?
DEGSY	What about it? You should have thought about that before you started auditioning for Wacky Races.
GREAVES	And then they both got out. It was as though they'd forgotten I was there.
CLIFF	How am I going to explain this down the garage?
GREAVES	I was bruised but in the bashing about a small tear had emerged in the bin bag.
DEGSY	Just tell them you had a fit or something.
CLIFF	What?

DEGSY   You forgot to take your medicine.

CLIFF   I'm not saying that.

DEGSY   I know someone who knows someone who knows a doctor who'll do all the paperwork for a few quid.

GREAVES   And I could see that in the crash the back door had bent open.

DEGSY   Look, I'm just trying to help you out.

CLIFF   Help me out? Help me out!? What's next? You going to strangle my mum's budgie?

GREAVES   And I managed to roll over to it, and push it open.

DEGSY   You ungrateful – oh fuck, I mean, I wasn't the one who swerved off the road because of Tiddles over there.

CLIFF   Oh fuck no.

DEGSY   Poor bloody Tiddles, poor bloody ex-mog.

GREAVES   And I was on the road, and the air felt good.

CLIFF   Jesus, what a mess.

GREAVES   And I started running.

DEGSY   You swerving across the road probably frightened him to death.

CLIFF   I don't know what I thought it was at first, but –

          (CLIFF taps DEGSY on the shoulder.)

CLIFF   It's, it's –

DEGSY   Him, he's, he's –

CLIFF/DEGSY   Legging it!

GREAVES   And I know they've seen me, but I'm fit, clean
               bill of health at the start of every season.

DEGSY   He's going for the great escape.

CLIFF   Degsy! He's running away.

DEGSY   And for a moment, a fleeting micro-moment, I
               think –

CLIFF   He's running away!

DEGSY   I am fucked, I am well fucked here.

CLIFF   Degsy, he's running away!

DEGSY   But then I realise there's only one thing to do.

CLIFF   And he looks really stupid, what with the bin
               bag, and his little legs going ten to the dozen.

DEGSY   After him.

CLIFF   What?

DEGSY   After him.

CLIFF   And Degsy is off after him.

DEGSY   Cliff! Don't just fucking stand there!

GREAVES   Obviously, given the bin bag, my escape is not
               as swift as it could have been, but I'm making
               good ground.

CLIFF   And the sight of Degsy, who probably hasn't
               done any physical exercise since 1985, and my
               van, and a dead cat . . .

               (*Beat.*)

CLIFF	And a fellar with a bin bag over his head legging it down a country road in the middle of nowhere.
	(*Beat.*)
CLIFF	I can't help thinking how did this come to pass? How did life get this complicated?
DEGSY	Cliff! What are you doing?
CLIFF	And then I think fuck it, I've come this far.
DEGSY	He's a nippy little bastard, but I've still got him in my sights.
GREAVES	The trouble is I can't see my feet.
CLIFF	I've come this far, I might as well have the full cardiac arrest.
DEGSY	He keeps veering all over the place.
GREAVES	And I notice a turn off, and a signpost.
CLIFF	So I fucking belt it.
DEGSY	And then he does a right.
GREAVES	There must be a village or something nearby.
CLIFF	I fucking super-propel it.
DEGSY	And I can't see him.
CLIFF	Linford Christie, eat your shorts.
GREAVES	Is that a village sign? Coming up? Over there?
DEGSY	And I'm thinking I am not up to this.
CLIFF	Eat your lycra lunchbox, sunshine!
DEGSY	And then there's Cliff –

CLIFF	Speedy Gonzalez on steroids, that's me.
DEGSY	He's, he's overtaking me?!
GREAVES	Yes, yes, it's a village, I can't read the name, but there's something.
DEGSY	He's sweating and huffing like a man possessed.
CLIFF	I am seriously going for it.
GREAVES	Where is everyone? There must be somebody about.
DEGSY	And I can hear Cliff repeating under his breath –
CLIFF	Come here Greaves, come here Greaves . . .
GREAVES	It's very hot and close inside the bin bag and one of them is getting nearer.
CLIFF	Come here Greaves.
GREAVES	I expect a rugby tackle any moment.
DEGSY	I don't believe it, he's going to catch him.
CLIFF	Yes!
DEGSY	He's going to do it –
GREAVES	Any moment.
CLIFF	For once in my life I'm going to achieve something!
DEGSY	And then –
CLIFF	Aaargh!
DEGSY	He stops.

(CLIFF *holds his chest.*)

CLIFF	There's this searing pain in my chest!
DEGSY	And he's away.
CLIFF	And I think, I think this is it.
DEGSY	Greaves is getting away.
CLIFF	Just a few seconds till I turn a nice shade of blue.
DEGSY	And then –
CLIFF	I have a vision, my funeral, an overhead view –
GREAVES	It's so hot inside this bag but I keep going
CLIFF	I'm being lowered into the ground –
DEGSY	And then –
GREAVES	Something underfoot.
DEGSY	He sort of slips and then –
GREAVES	The earth gives way.
DEGSY	He does this forward roll –
GREAVES	A tumble into the dark.
DEGSY	And he smacks his head on the road.
GREAVES	Ow!
DEGSY	And he's laid out.
GREAVES	And I think –
DEGSY	The bastard has knocked himself out again!
GREAVES	Bugger.

(*Beat.*)

CLIFF   And then the pain starts to fade.

DEGSY   And he is, he's unconscious.

(CLIFF *has started to recover from his seizure.*)

CLIFF   And Degsy is standing there.

DEGSY   Oi, Cliff!

CLIFF   He's shouting –

DEGSY   Dog-shit.

CLIFF   What?

DEGSY   Dog-shit. He slipped on some dog-shit.

(*Stage goes into darkness. Dim light on* GREAVES.)

GREAVES   I was beginning to get quite used to darkness. But the thing is, when there are different shades of darkness, different tones, different . . . and this darkness, it was a blood-red darkness, it was still a darkness, but it was, it's difficult to describe, but there was someone there, in the darkness, there was a presence. I'm not saying, no, I'm not saying that, no no no, not, no not, but there was something there with me, there was, and, and it felt, yes, yes I am saying, I am saying that I was being protected, somehow, by somebody, I felt, safe.

(*The atmosphere is broken.*)

DEGSY   After Greaves had up-ended himself on the dog-shit.

GREAVES   But then the darkness ended, and –

CLIFF	I realised it was a stitch.
GREAVES	I . . . I was in a church?
CLIFF	We picked him up.
DEGSY	Just as a car drove past.
CLIFF	We pretended to be a gang of pissheads.

(They pretend to be pissheads.)

GREAVES	Yes, definitely, a church.
DEGSY	And I'm thinking –
CLIFF	I'm giving up thinking it's not good for you.
DEGSY	I'm thinking, what now? What the fuck now?
CLIFF	I just want to lie down.
DEGSY	And then there's –
CLIFF	Anywhere.
DEGSY	This church.
CLIFF	It's all bordered up and got a for sale sign up but –
DEGSY	It's easy to break in.
CLIFF	And we have to carry Greaves.
DEGSY	He still hasn't come round.
CLIFF	And he's moaning and saying things.
DEGSY	Nothing I could make out.
CLIFF	And we dump him on this pile of old carpets.
GREAVES	There was this overwhelming mustiness.

DEGSY	And Cliff finds this batch of candles.
CLIFF	It looks quite cosy though, I say so myself –
DEGSY	And I figure I need to get my act together, I need to get my shit collected.
CLIFF	And Degsy gets out his pocket radio.
	(*They listen.*)
CLIFF	The reception is not great.
DEGSY	And fuck me –
CLIFF	It's like in one of those crap TV things when they switch on the radio and they're talking about what you want to hear straightaway.
DEGSY	It's on the news.
CLIFF	Not the local either.
DEGSY	The national friggin' news!
CLIFF	And apparently –
DEGSY	I knew, I knew, I *knew* I was doing the right thing –
CLIFF	Apparently –
DEGSY	There are hundreds –
CLIFF	That's what they said –
DEGSY	Hundreds of people, punters, fans, ordinary joes, they're having this, this demonstration outside the ground.
CLIFF	Hundreds?

DEGSY   And they're saying I've done the right thing,
               enough is enough, and that I should be given a
               let-off and the game should be replayed.

CLIFF   Not that they know who has done it.

DEGSY   But then they say they are looking –

CLIFF   For two fellars –

DEGSY   And –

CLIFF   A white van –

DEGSY   To help –

CLIFF   Oh, fuck –

DEGSY   The police with their inquiries.

CLIFF   Oh, fucking fuck –

DEGSY   And then there's this discussion, this phone-
               in, and it's about us, about what we've done –

CLIFF   My fucking van –

DEGSY   And sure there are a few wankers going on,
               saying I was this, this hooligan, this
               disrespecter of the law, but there were also
               loads of people –

CLIFF   My fucking van with my fucking name and
               fucking phone number –

DEGSY   Giving me the thumbs up, saying what I'd done
               was, was, about time, that's what they seemed
               to be saying –

CLIFF   Sprayed across the fucking side of it!

DEGSY   I was a hero. I was a hero of the people.

GREAVES   What?

(*Beat.*)

DEGSY   You heard.

GREAVES   I don't think so.

DEGSY   I do think so.

             (*Beat.*)

DEGSY   Thought we'd bring you somewhere you felt at
             home.

             (*Beat.*)

DEGSY   What do you think? Bit of a sad dump, innit?

             (*Beat.*)

DEGSY   Not speaking, are we?

             (*Beat.*)

DEGSY   Not giving nothing away, eh?

GREAVES   I have nothing to say.

DEGSY   Aha, you spoke, I made you speak, you didn't
             want to, and I made you.

GREAVES   This is pathetic, this is –

DEGSY   Where's your God now, then? Eh? Eh?

GREAVES   He's here.

DEGSY   Is he?

GREAVES   Yes.

DEGSY   Well he's keeping a low fucking profile.

GREAVES   How, how could you possibly understand?

CLIFF   Degsy?

DEGSY   Oi, God, you wanker, if you're so big and mighty, why don't you do me? Eh?

CLIFF   Degsy?

DEGSY   Come on God, thunderbolt me if you're hard enough. You're on home turf mate, home advantage, should be a walkover, you, all-knowing all-powerful mysterious force, versus me, some oikky pleb with no O-levels.

CLIFF   Degsy?

DEGSY   Oi, God! Oi?! I'm talking to you. Oi!?

CLIFF   Degsy?

DEGSY   Now that is the problem with God, he never answers. He thinks he's so big, he can't be bothered to put himself out.

CLIFF   Degsy?

DEGSY   All that fucking praying they make you do as a kid, and he never bothers talking back, not even a whisper, not even the slightest –

CLIFF   Degsy?!

DEGSY   What? What is it?

               (*Beat.*)

CLIFF   I was thinking.

DEGSY   Yea and?

CLIFF   I was thinking, I, I might, I might, pop off for a bit.

DEGSY   Eh?

CLIFF   Get out of your hair.

DEGSY   Are you –

CLIFF   I'll come back, don't worry, honest, I wouldn't just, you know –

DEGSY   Eh? Cliff, what is this, are you saying –

CLIFF   You know? I won't be long, I'm not going to do –

DEGSY   What?

CLIFF   Do a runner.

            (*Beat.*)

DEGSY   Do a runner?

CLIFF   No, the thought hadn't even entered my head.

DEGSY   Hadn't it?

CLIFF   No.

            (*Beat.*)

DEGSY   Still no sign, then? But then I suppose he's a busy fellar, you know, what with being God and all that.

CLIFF   I'll be off, then?

DEGSY   Not even a shaft of light? Poor friggin' show if you ask me. Is he always this unreliable?

CLIFF   I won't be long.

DEGSY   No, Cliff.

CLIFF   I'm just going to stretch my legs. Hey, I could bring back some crisps.

DEGSY   Cliff, no. You are not going anywhere.

CLIFF   I don't know about you, but I'm starving –

DEGSY   You are not going anywhere.

CLIFF   Or what about a carry out?

DEGSY   We're staying here.

CLIFF   What do you fancy? Chinese? Indian?

DEGSY   We are staying here.

             (*Beat.*)

CLIFF   And then what? We stay here, and then what?

             (*Beat.*)

CLIFF   Degsy? And then what? We stay here, and
             then . . . I don't get it, we stay here, and then
             . . . what!!? What happens after the staying
             here bit?!

DEGSY   I am a hero, Cliff.

CLIFF   I know you are, Degs.

DEGSY   There are thousands of people out there,
             supporting what I've done.

CLIFF   Eh? Hold on, thousands?

DEGSY   Yea, thousands of people making a stand for
             me.

CLIFF   No, hundreds, not thousands, hundreds.

DEGSY   Eh? What are you saying?

CLIFF   I'm just saying it's not thousands, it's
             hundreds –

DEGSY	How do you know?
CLIFF	That's what they said on the radio.
DEGSY	Well that's the media, they're not going to tell you truth are they?
CLIFF	Why not?
DEGSY	Because, because . . . it's a conspiracy Cliff, they want us out the game. The regular fan with the season ticket, we're no fucking use to them.
CLIFF	What?
DEGSY	This is me saying, you can't get rid of us that fucking easy.
CLIFF	Degsy . . .
DEGSY	This is me saying, we're here whether you, mister fucking corporate fucking bullshit, whether you want us or not, we're still turning up.
CLIFF	OK Degs, I see your point, mate –
DEGSY	Me and all those thousands and thousands of others –
CLIFF	How many times, it's not thousands –
DEGSY	You think I don't know what I'm doing don't you?
CLIFF	No I'm just saying –

(DEGSY *suddenly turns his attention to* GREAVES.)

DEGSY	Hey where is he? I thought God was making a special guest appearance?

CLIFF   Degs . . .

DEGSY   But then that would be going against two
             thousand years of tradition, wouldn't it? You
             see, that's the problem with God, it's all
             bullshit.

CLIFF   Are you OK, Degs? Are you alright? Degs?

DEGSY   You would have thought, wouldn't you, you
             know, what with him being God, that he would
             think, oh yea, I'll just fucking turn up one day,
             yea, why not, prove once and for all that it's
             not just some mad fucking lie that's got out of
             hand.

CLIFF   Degsy!

             (DEGSY *looks at* CLIFF.)

DEGSY   I've got a plan, everything is going exactly to
             order, everything is working out nicely.

CLIFF   I know you have, Degs.

DEGSY   Everything is hunky-dory, hokey-cokey.

CLIFF   I know it is, Degs, I know it is.

DEGSY   Sweet as a nut.

             (*Beat.*)

CLIFF   And I thought, he's lost it, I mean, I thought
             he'd lost it before, but this was losing it, you
             know what I mean, this was –

DEGSY   (*to himself*) It was a goal, that goal, not a
             goal . . .

CLIFF   Losing it, lost it, where-is-it-can't-fucking-find-
             it losing it.

             (*Beat.*)

DEGSY	Say it was a goal.
GREAVES	What do you possibly hope to achieve . . .
DEGSY	It was a goal.
GREAVES	No.
DEGSY	Yes.
GREAVES	No.
DEGSY	Yes.
GREAVES	No.
DEGSY	Yes.
CLIFF	To be honest it didn't seem like much of a plan.
DEGSY	How do you get out of bed in the morning?
GREAVES	What?
DEGSY	Everyone hates you.
GREAVES	I like to think of it as respect.
DEGSY	I hate you.
GREAVES	Do you really? What a surprise.
DEGSY	All that hate, fuck me, you must be sick.
GREAVES	Sick? Me? Have you looked in the mirror recently?
DEGSY	Say it was a goal.
GREAVES	No.
DEGSY	Just say.

GREAVES   No.

DEGSY   It was a goal.

GREAVES   No.

DEGSY   Just say.

                 (*They repeat this exchange, should feel like a
                 long time, until:*)

GREAVES   OK, IT WAS A GOAL.

DEGSY   Just say.

GREAVES   It was a goal!!

                 (*Silence.*)

GREAVES   It was a goal.

                 (*Silence.*)

DEGSY   Say it was a goal and mean it.

GREAVES   It was a goal.

DEGSY   I said, and mean it.

GREAVES   It was a goal.

DEGSY   That doesn't sound any different.

GREAVES   It was a goal.

DEGSY   I said, with meaning, not louder, with meaning,
                 as though you mean it.

GREAVES   It was a goal.

CLIFF   He seems to be saying it was a goal, Degs.

DEGSY   You stay out of this.

GREAVES	It was a goal.
DEGSY	And you can shut up, you're just taking the piss now.
GREAVES	It was a goal.
DEGSY	I said shut up.
GREAVES	It was a goal. I made a mistake, oh dear, oh dear.
DEGSY	Oi!
GREAVES	What a silly referee . . .
DEGSY	Oi, you don't seem to realise I could do something very nasty –
GREAVES	Oh, whatever next? I'm so frightened.
DEGSY	I could, I could cut your ear off, mate.
GREAVES	That old cliché.
CLIFF	Oh, Jesus.
GREAVES	I might wet myself I'm so scared.
CLIFF	Oh no, we don't want him pissing his pants.
DEGSY	And we'll put it in the post.
CLIFF	Degsy?
DEGSY	Send it in a box to your nearest and dearest.
GREAVES	Can't you think of anything original –
DEGSY	Right, you've fucking asked for it –
CLIFF	No, Degsy, no –
DEGSY	Cliff, what have you got?

CLIFF	Degsy!
	(*Beat.*)
CLIFF	And we stood there looking at each other.
DEGSY	What is it Clifford?
CLIFF	I, I don't think –
DEGSY	What?
CLIFF	And at that moment I didn't know what to say, I was out of ideas, up a dead-end.
DEGSY	What is it Cliff?
CLIFF	And then in the silence, in the distance.
	(*Silence.*)
CLIFF	We could all hear it. Unmistakable.
GREAVES	The cavalry.
DEGSY	That's miles away.
CLIFF	It was some way off.
	(*They listen.*)
CLIFF	And then we listened to it disappear.
	(*Silence.*)
CLIFF	Christ knows what the time was.
GREAVES	It must have been past midnight.
CLIFF	I was shagged, knackered, and worn out.
GREAVES	All you could hear was the wind.

CLIFF	In that order.
GREAVES	He tried listening to the radio.
CLIFF	But the reception seemed to be going.
DEGSY	I bet they're putting out a signal.
CLIFF	You couldn't make anything out.
DEGSY	I bet they're putting out a signal to interfere with the airwaves.

(*Beat.*)

CLIFF	I resisted asking who they were.

(*Beat.*)

CLIFF	Greaves seemed to have nodded off.
DEGSY	Why don't you get your head down?
CLIFF	No, I couldn't sleep, not in here.
DEGSY	Get some rest.
CLIFF	No, no, I don't feel like it.
DEGSY	Whatever.

(*Silence. Suspicion.*)

CLIFF	I didn't want to go to sleep. I was thinking, I'll let Degsy nod off, he must be more knackered than me.
DEGSY	Alright, mate?
CLIFF	Yea, yea mate, alright.

(*Beat.*)

CLIFF	And then I'll fuck off.

DEGSY   There was no way I was going to go to sleep.

CLIFF   Got to stay awake.

DEGSY   No way, got to keep going.

CLIFF   Keep me wits about me.

DEGSY   Can't trust anyone.

CLIFF   Stay on the case.

               (CLIFF *falls asleep.*)

DEGSY   And then there was this noise. Outside. I look
               over and they're both out of it. And then, there
               it is again. Someone's out there.

               (*Beat.*)

DEGSY   And I'm thinking, keep it calm, it's just some
               local, and there it is again.

               (*Beat.*)

DEGSY   And, and I start edging towards the door, and
               I'm thinking this is dumb, this is –

               (*Beat.*)

DEGSY   And it's there again, followed by, sounds like
               someone's scraping their fingernails, and fuck,
               there's a knock at the door, and I'm, Jesus
               Christ there's someone out there. Oi! Who is
               it?

GREAVES   I come to, and, and the wind, I'm very aware of
               the wind and –

DEGSY   'Who's there?', I'm shouting. 'Who's there?'

GREAVES   Towards the front of the church, something –

CLIFF	And I startle to, and, what, where's Degsy? And, oh no, Greaves –
DEGSY	'Who's there?'
GREAVES	Someone, shouting.
CLIFF	Oh fuck, where is he?
DEGSY	And I pull the church door open –
GREAVES	And I make towards whatever it is –
CLIFF	Oi, Greaves, where are you?
DEGSY	And I'm outside and it's dark –
GREAVES	And it's cold –
CLIFF	It's fucking freezing –
DEGSY	And –
GREAVES	I have no idea what's in front of me.
CLIFF	I wish I'd brought me torch.
DEGSY	My stomach's in my mouth.
CLIFF	And I can't see a thing.
GREAVES	But then there's a surge –
DEGSY	A push –
CLIFF	Oi, something's happening here –
GREAVES	Where is this?
CLIFF	Hey what's going on?
GREAVES	There are lights –
DEGSY	And this feeling I thought was fear, it's not –

GREAVES   Of course –

CLIFF   And I catch a smell of something –

GREAVES   Of course, the lights at the end of the tunnel –

CLIFF   Bovril? Someone, someone's drinking bovril!

DEGSY   And I think, I know this feeling, I –

CLIFF/DEGSY   I know where this is.

GREAVES   The noise –

CLIFF   It's getting louder –

GREAVES   And louder –

DEGSY   There is only one noise like that –

CLIFF   It could burst your eardrums –

GREAVES   The energy –

DEGSY   The sheer fucking buzz –

GREAVES   You have to experience it to understand it –

CLIFF   It's the game, it's –

DEGSY   Oh, yes –

CLIFF/DEGSY   It's the match –

GREAVES   The floodlights –

DEGSY   The green of the pitch –

CLIFF   And you are not going to believe this –

DEGSY   I'm running out with the teams –

CLIFF	I'm the ref, I'm done up as the ref, the shorts, everything –
GREAVES	And the game kicks off –
CLIFF	I'm the ref, and I'm running about, over here, over there, doing that nifty backward thing that refs do –
DEGSY	And I notice, on the touchline, it is, yea, it's Phillippa –
CLIFF	And then there's this incident off the ball –
GREAVES	I couldn't see it clearly –
DEGSY	And I think I'll show her, show her what I can do –
CLIFF	And, hey it's Brickie, and he's complaining, swearing his head off, and I think I'm not having this, I'm the ref!
GREAVES	But the floodlights, they're so bright –
DEGSY	She'll want me back then, oh yes, she'll have me back –
GREAVES	And the game seems a long way away –
CLIFF	I'm not having this, and I reach into my top pocket, and –
DEGSY	Hey, what's happening?
CLIFF	I pull out a red card –
DEGSY	I'm being sent off –
GREAVES	I can sense people getting angry –
CLIFF	Go on, early bath, you great slobbering fat arse!

DEGSY   What have I done?

CLIFF   And I think, I like this!

DEGSY   I haven't done anything!

CLIFF   And he's got tears rolling down his ugly mug.

DEGSY   And I have to leave the pitch, and, Phillippa,
             she's not there.

GREAVES   I can feel the hatred, the ugliness –

CLIFF   And then I send off the old dear with the
             stethoscope from downstairs for a late tackle –

GREAVES   Coming towards me –

DEGSY   I can't see her anywhere –

CLIFF   And everyone starts crowding round me,
             questioning my decision –

GREAVES   Faces jeering and pointing –

CLIFF   But the more they complain, the more I send
             off –

DEGSY   And it's impossible to get through, but I can
             see her, she's there, I can see her, and I try and
             shout over the top –

GREAVES   Screaming at me –

DEGSY   I love you, I love you –

CLIFF   And the crowd are on the pitch, and I start
             sending all them off, too.

DEGSY   And I can't get through, there are too many
             people –

GREAVES   Bearing down on me –

CLIFF   Red card!

DEGSY   I'm pushing –

CLIFF   Red card!

GREAVES   I prepare myself –

CLIFF   Red card, red card!

DEGSY   I'm pushing harder and harder –

CLIFF   And I keep going until I've sent every last
             person off, off the pitch, out of the ground, and
             I'm standing there, with me red card, and the
             whole ground is . . . empty.

GREAVES   Desolate.

DEGSY   Vanished, everyone's vanished, except –

CLIFF   Oh, yes.

DEGSY   There's Phillippa.

CLIFF   A job well done.

             (*Snap out on* CLIFF.)

DEGSY   And I go towards her, but she won't look at
             me, and I, I try to remember what it was I
             wanted to say to her.

GREAVES   And the floodlights, they snap off, and once
             again I'm crouched there in the darkness.

DEGSY   And I can't remember any of it, and she just
             turns away and walks off.

GREAVES   And I, I try to feel, I try to find the, the person,
             my special friend, the one who is always there –

DEGSY   And I'm helpless, I'm tongue-tied, dumb, and
                 she just goes, she doesn't even look back, she
                 just –

GREAVES   He isn't there.

DEGSY   Fucks off.

GREAVES   There is no one there.

DEGSY   Doesn't even look back.

GREAVES   And it hits me –

DEGSY   I feel sick.

GREAVES   Fear.

DEGSY   Sicker than I've ever felt, ever.

                 (*Silence. Lighting change. Back to the
                 church.*)

DEGSY   (*half-shout*) Phillip . . . a.

GREAVES   Ah yes, that was the dream.

DEGSY   And then I realise –

GREAVES   This isn't.

                 (CLIFF *snores.*)

DEGSY   Cliff's snoring.

GREAVES   There's the beginning of a new day.

DEGSY   It's cold.

GREAVES   Freezing.

                 (*Beat.*)

GREAVES   I can make out the vague remnant of a stained glass window.

DEGSY   (*soft*) Oi, Greaves . . .

GREAVES   Nothing spectacular, but it reminds me of the church where we got married.

DEGSY   Oi, Greaves.

            (*Beat.*)

GREAVES   Yes?

            (*Beat.*)

GREAVES   Yes? What do you want?

            (*Beat.*)

DEGSY   Nothing. Just checking.

GREAVES   He fiddles with his radio. But it's very definitely dead.

DEGSY   Fuck.

GREAVES   There's a strange awkwardness to him.

            (*Beat.*)

DEGSY   Who buys a church?

GREAVES   What?

DEGSY   Who'd want to buy a church? What are you going to do with it? Start your own religion?

            (*Beat.*)

GREAVES   People do them up and live them.

DEGSY   Live in them?

GREAVES   Apparently.

               (*Beat.*)

DEGSY   People shouldn't live in churches. I mean,
               churches are for . . . people should get married
               in churches.

               (*Beat.*)

DEGSY   Are you, are you married?

GREAVES   I don't think that's any of your business.

DEGSY   Alright, I'm not that arsed.

               (*Beat.*)

GREAVES   I suppose I still am. Technically.

               (*Beat.*)

DEGSY   I got the local radio to read it out.

GREAVES   Read what out?

DEGSY   You know, the proposal. On air. That wanker
               who's on in the afternoon. Thought it would be
               a laugh. And then they phoned her up at work,
               to see what she was going to say.

               (*Beat.*)

DEGSY   She, she declined. You must be joking, she
               said. And I was at work. With all me mates.
               They . . . they found it quite amusing. You
               know what mates are like. Might as well have
               got a sign saying 'loser' and hung it round my
               neck. You see, I thought it was a way of
               getting her back. I thought women liked all that
               big romantic bullshit, but no, it would appear
               not. I fucked up yet again. I ballsed it up grand
               style. Not if you paid me a thousand pounds.
               She said that as well. And the DJ goes, 'cause

he's having a right laugh by now, he goes,
what about a million, and she says, no not even
fifteen million, and they fucking fell about.
Fifteen million? What's that about? Where did
that come from? Not twelve or sixteen or . . .
fifteen. They fell about . . . not even . . . fuck.

(*Beat.*)

GREAVES   Why don't you ask for forgiveness?

DEGSY   Eh?

GREAVES   Ask God to forgive you.

(*Beat.*)

GREAVES   If God forgives you, maybe it'll be easier for
Phillippa to forgive you.

(*Beat.*)

GREAVES   I've always found he understands.

DEGSY   Understands what?

GREAVES   Human error. Fallibility.

DEGSY   Sicker than I've ever felt, ever.

GREAVES   Why don't you try?

(*Beat.*)

DEGSY   Get out of it.

GREAVES   What's to lose, Degsy?

(*Beat.*)

GREAVES   Degsy, what's to lose?

DEGSY   What, what sort of thing do I say?

GREAVES   You don't have to say anything.

DEGSY   Shall I, do I have to kneel?

GREAVES   It's not obligatory, but it can help.

           (DEGSY *kneels.*)

CLIFF   It was about now that I woke up, and, I'm a bit groggy, and –

DEGSY   What now?

CLIFF   And I can make out . . . and I think this is a bit odd –

DEGSY   What do I do now?

CLIFF   This is a bit fucking bizarre.

GREAVES   Just, try and feel his presence.

           (DEGSY *prays. Shuts his eyes.* CLIFF *approaches.*)

CLIFF   Degsy?

DEGSY   Yea?

CLIFF   Degsy? What are you doing?

DEGSY   Fuck me, is that –

           (DEGSY *stops. He realises that* CLIFF *is not the voice of God.*)

DEGSY   What are you doing?

CLIFF   No, what are you doing?

DEGSY   What am I doing?

CLIFF   Yea, what are you doing?

DEGSY	What am I doing!?
CLIFF	Yes, what are you doing?
DEGSY	Shit, shit, this is, fuck, what *am* I doing?
CLIFF	Exactly, what are you doing?
DEGSY	I've, I've been hoodwinked.
CLIFF	Eh?
DEGSY	Oh yes, very clever, very smart Greaves, you thought you had me there, didn't you?
CLIFF	And Degsy started to, Degsy, Degsy, what are you doing?
DEGSY	None of your business.
CLIFF	Degsy?
DEGSY	None of your fucking business.
CLIFF	And he yanked him up.
DEGSY	You are going to pay, Greaves.
CLIFF	And he threw him to the ground. Degsy, Degsy, this is not clever.
DEGSY	Crawl Greaves, crawl in the fucking dirt.
CLIFF	And he kicked him.
DEGSY	Where you belong.
CLIFF	This is, this is getting way out of hand Degs, Degsy . . .
DEGSY	Scum.
CLIFF	And I go to stop him –

DEGSY   Get out of it!

CLIFF   And we struggle –

DEGSY   Get off!

CLIFF   And he elbows me in the face –

DEGSY   Stay out of this, Cliff –

CLIFF   Stop this Degsy –

DEGSY   Fuck off!

CLIFF   What are you doing?

DEGSY   What am I doing? I'm doing *him*, that's what
               I'm doing. I'm doing mister hard-but-fair.

CLIFF   But Degsy –

DEGSY   Oh yes, here it comes –

CLIFF   But Degsy –

DEGSY   (*mimics*) But Degsy, you don't want to hurt
               him, oh no, you don't want to do that!

CLIFF   But Degsy, it's only a game.

               (*Pause.*)

DEGSY   What?

CLIFF   It's only a game, it's only fucking football.

DEGSY   I don't believe you just said that, Cliff.

CLIFF   But it is.

DEGSY   Only, only a game?

CLIFF   It's not as though it means . . . anything.

DEGSY   That's the sort of shit I've come to expect from you, Cliff. The sort of half-cocked bollocks I know you will always trot out. And if I've told you once, I've told you a fucking million times, this is about saying, it's saying you people are taking the piss, and I'm –

CLIFF   Bollocks, this is all about Phillippa. You fucked it up with her.

DEGSY   What?

CLIFF   You fucked up with her, so –

DEGSY   Cliff, it wasn't a goal, how many times –

CLIFF   So you do this.

DEGSY   And how dare you fucking mention Phillippa!?

CLIFF   You've always been a mad bastard but this is madder and, and more bastard than anything –

DEGSY   You think you're a fucking psychiatrist now, don't you? Eh?

CLIFF   Yea, I do it cash-in-hand when I haven't got any decorating.

DEGSY   This is all about Phillippa?! You've got a fucking nerve. Who, who are you to start giving me –

CLIFF   I don't know why I always give you the time of day Degsy, I should have just gone to bed.

DEGSY   You are talking about the woman I love.

CLIFF   The woman you love?

DEGSY   Yea.

CLIFF   The woman you love?

DEGSY   Yes, yes, the woman –

CLIFF   The woman you love?

DEGSY   Yea, yea the woman –

CLIFF   I love. The woman he loves, the woman I love,
             Phillippa, the woman –

DEGSY   Why is it with you Cliff, you can't just say
             something once. Yes, the woman I love!

CLIFF   OK, OK, so, is that why you were knocking off
             that schoolgirl?

DEGSY   Eh?

CLIFF   You know what I'm talking about.

DEGSY   And . . . she wasn't a schoolgirl, she was a
             student.

CLIFF   Same fucking difference.

             (*They retreat from each other, and then* DEGSY
             realises something.)

DEGSY   How do you know about that?

             (DEGSY *stares at* CLIFF.)

DEGSY   Cliff, how do you know about that?

CLIFF   I have been meaning to say actually, Degs.

DEGSY   Say what? What are you on about?

CLIFF   I have been meaning to mention it actually,
             don't know why I haven't –

DEGSY   What?

CLIFF   She just turned up. One night, at mine.

DEGSY	Who did?
CLIFF	Phillippa.
	(*Beat.*)
DEGSY	When?
CLIFF	After one of your rows, she was really upset, and –
DEGSY	Eh, what, why didn't you tell me about this?
CLIFF	Well, we don't ever talk about things like that, do we?
DEGSY	She turned up at yours?
CLIFF	Yea, you hadn't come home the night before or something, and she was, she was saying, she just happened to mention, because she was very upset –
DEGSY	What?
CLIFF	We just had a cup of tea, that's all. Just a cup of tea.
DEGSY	Eh?
CLIFF	Honest. Cross my heart, honest Degs, no word of a lie.
DEGSY	Is there something you're not telling me?
CLIFF	No.
DEGSY	Cliff, you, you fucking better not have?
CLIFF	No.
DEGSY	No what?
	(*Beat.*)

CLIFF   I didn't want to –

DEGSY   Eh?

CLIFF   She said she just wanted a cuddle.

DEGSY   A . . . a cuddle?

CLIFF   Honest to God, Degs, that's what she said,
give me a cuddle, and you know how it is,
women they're always saying stuff like that.

DEGSY   She said she just wanted a cuddle?

CLIFF   Yea.

DEGSY   A cuddle?

CLIFF   And then it just happened.

DEGSY   What?

CLIFF   I didn't want it to happen, I didn't say no, but
it did happen, it happened, there I've fucking
said it, it happened, you must know how it is,
one minute we're just being mates, and the
next –

DEGSY   You utter, total bastard.

CLIFF   And then in the morning, I realised –

DEGSY   In the morning? In the morning?

CLIFF   I realised, listen to me Degs, I realised that
she'd just used me –

DEGSY   Oh dear, poor little you.

CLIFF   She'd just used me to get at you.

DEGSY   Well she's fucking succeeded, then.

CLIFF	And to be honest I didn't enjoy it that much.
DEGSY	What?
CLIFF	I just kept thinking of you.
DEGSY	Eh?
CLIFF	I felt really guilty.
DEGSY	So, not only do you sleep with the woman I love –
CLIFF	That's nothing against Phillippa! Honest Degs, she's got a great –

(CLIFF *stops just there.*)

CLIFF	Oh shit.
DEGSY	You've even got the fucking nerve not to enjoy it?

(*Silence.*)

CLIFF	I thought about saying sorry.
DEGSY	And I thought you were my mate.
CLIFF	But I didn't think it would do any good.

(*Silence.*)

DEGSY	And I thought, I've never liked living much anyway. I've never seen what all the fuss was about. Beer, telly, shagging, footie, what else is there? It's a piss-poor selection of alternatives. It's a friggin' threadbare variety packed full of fuck all and fuck all. I mean, what is the point, what is the point, in even bothering to reach up and take it off the shelf? What is the fucking point?
CLIFF	And Degsy was off –

DEGSY	What is the fucking point? Your starter for ten.
CLIFF	Up the aisle –
GREAVES	Out of the church.
DEGSY	Over the edge.
CLIFF	And he's outside –
GREAVES	The daylight, it's quite strong now.
DEGSY	Nothing to hold on to.
GREAVES	It's quite a shock to the system.
CLIFF	And he's running through all these graves –
GREAVES	It's very overgrown.
CLIFF	But they're still someone's grave.
DEGSY	What do they care? They're dead, aren't they?
GREAVES	And there was a man jogging.
CLIFF	And Degsy, he's heading across this road –
GREAVES	It seemed strange, someone doing something normal.
DEGSY	Fuck all and fuck all.
CLIFF	And there's a pond, a duck pond, not that it's full of ducks, but you get the picture.
GREAVES	And he stopped and watched as –
CLIFF	Degsy just waded in, up to his knees –
DEGSY	What else is there?
CLIFF	Up to his waist –

GREAVES   And then he seemed to just fling himself –

CLIFF   He went under –

GREAVES   And he stayed under –

CLIFF   Degsy!

GREAVES   He didn't seem to be coming back up.

CLIFF   Degsy!

           (*Blackout. Fade up on* DEGSY *sitting on chair.*)

DEGSY   That goal. Not a goal. Truth. Absolute.

CLIFF   (*off*) Through here, OK, thanks.

           (CLIFF *enters.*)

CLIFF   And do you know, it wasn't. A goal. Well, it
           was a goal, but, it happened that, look this is a
           bit convoluted so stay with me.

DEGSY   What do you want?

CLIFF   I was passing, thought I'd drop by, say hello.

DEGSY   Hello.

           (*Beat.*)

CLIFF   Hey, it's not a bad little, er, room this, is it?

           (*Awkward.*)

CLIFF   So, what was I saying, the goal, I tell you, you
           couldn't write this, it turned out that our
           goalie, the one who got his fingertips to it, the
           one with the unusual . . . well it was revealed –

DEGSY   If there is one thing that football has taught
           me, never –

CLIFF   Never trust a goalie with dyed-orange hair.

               (*Beat.*)

CLIFF   Anyway, as I was saying, it was revealed, in
               fact splashed all over the front pages, that, he,
               the goalie, our goalie, he had actually been
               given a bung –

DEGSY   Not a goal.

CLIFF   That is, a very sizeable donation to his bank
               account in respect of him throwing the match.
               There was video evidence, a couple of phone
               calls, it did not look good. And oh yea, by the
               way, Degsy, he didn't drown.

DEGSY   Greaves –

CLIFF   Greaves saved him.

DEGSY   Bastard.

CLIFF   Yea, he got me to untie him, and then he
               jumped in, dragged him out, and gave him the
               kiss of life.

               (*Awkward moment.*)

CLIFF   So, our goalie is all over the paper, Degsy is all
               over the paper, Phillippa sells this old picture
               of him looking like some sort of axe murderer in
               a shower cap and it's on the front of every
               tabloid, and he becomes known as Mad –

DEGSY   Cow –

CLIFF   Bastard. You can even buy a t-shirt with said
               picture outside the ground on game days.

DEGSY   I was doing the right thing.

CLIFF   I know you were.

DEGSY   I was.

CLIFF   I know you were Degs, I know you were.

               (*Beat.*)

CLIFF   Anyway, as you can imagine, it all got very complicated, and to cut a very very long story short the clubs actually decided to replay the game. Unprecedented, but that's what they decide to do.

DEGSY   Don't let me keep you.

CLIFF   Yea, it's just I, I've got to get off to my community service.

DEGSY   How nice for you.

CLIFF   I'm helping out this old couple, trimming their hedge, weeding, thought I might even have a go at their fence. They're very nice, for . . . for old people. They make me feel quite at home. Did I say, they've, they've got Sky?

               (*Beat.*)

CLIFF   They said I can go round to watch the match if I want.

               (*Beat.*)

CLIFF   It's alright, gardening, quite satisfying. Gardening, hey, apparently it's the new rock 'n' roll.

DEGSY   What?

CLIFF   Just an article I read. As a metaphor, I don't think it holds much water. You may have gathered that the authorities were a bit more lenient towards me. Sometimes it pays to be the sap, the sidekick.

DEGSY   The bastard saved me.

CLIFF   Greaves did visit Degsy once. It was for a
             paper who'd bought Greaves' story.

             (GREAVES *enters. They stand very awkward in
             each other's presence.*)

GREAVES   Thought I'd come and, and –

             (GREAVES *makes to shake hands.* DEGSY *turns
             away.*)

GREAVES   No hard feelings.

             (*Beat.*)

GREAVES   Obviously they couldn't take a picture of us
             together, so they took one of me outside,
             making a discreet exit.

CLIFF   "Secret Visit by Kidnap Ref."

DEGSY   Bastard.

GREAVES   I don't know what I expected, I suppose, if I'm
             honest, maybe . . . maybe a thank you.

DEGSY   He never had the bottle to say he fucked up,
             that goal, not a goal.

             (*Beat.*)

GREAVES   I didn't stay long. They wanted to re-do me
             coming out of the . . . the . . . what do you call
             it, the gate, and that was that. I can't say I
             didn't feel guilty about the money, I did. But I
             am going to put it to good use. I've been asked
             to go overseas, to pass on my experience of the
             game. And do you know, that day I had a very
             strong, intuitive feeling of a phase in my life
             drawing to a close, and a new one beginning.
             This had been a test, and I had come through.

For a moment things had looked bleak, but
those moments they are part of the journey,
part of the test, and I knew, my belief was
stronger than ever. Much, much stronger.

(GREAVES *starts to exit.*)

DEGSY   (*quiet*) Knobhead.

(GREAVES *exits, smugger than ever.*)

CLIFF   OK Degs, I'll . . . I'll see you soon, mate.

(CLIFF *starts to exit.*)

CLIFF   Hey, did you read about that local drama
          group, they're doing a musical about us.

(*Beat.*)

CLIFF   And as I was leaving I was reflecting, mulling
          over, thinking about everything that had
          happened, I was strolling through the park
          actually, there were a few leaves were falling,
          and I was weighing up all that I'd been
          through, and . . . I thought, on the one hand
          you've got football, and then on the other,
          you've got real life. Football, real life. Real life,
          football. And I was thinking, you should
          always keep it like that.

(*Football crowd cheering.* CLIFF *has started to
exit, but then turns back, and signals for it to
stop.*)

CLIFF   Oh yea, the replay.

(*Beat.*)

CLIFF   We lost. One-nil. Looked offside to me.

(CLIFF *and* DEGSY *look at each other.
Blackout.*)